PREVENTION AND CONTROL OF
COVID-19

PREVENTION AND CONTROL OF
COVID-19

Editor-in-chief

Wenhong Zhang

Huashan Hospital of Fudan University, China

NEW JERSEY · LONDON · SINGAPORE · BEIJING · SHANGHAI · HONG KONG · TAIPEI · CHENNAI · TOKYO

Published by

World Century Publishing Corp.
27 Warren Street
Suite 401-402
Hackensack, NJ 07601
USA

and

World Scientific Publishing Co. Pte. Ltd.
5 Toh Tuck Link, Singapore 596224
USA office: 27 Warren Street, Suite 401-402, Hackensack, NJ 07601
UK office: 57 Shelton Street, Covent Garden, London WC2H 9HE

British Library Cataloguing-in-Publication Data
A catalogue record for this book is available from the British Library.

张文宏教授支招防控新型冠状病毒
Originally published in Chinese by Shanghai Scientific and Technical Publishers
Copyright © Shanghai Scientific and Technical Publishers 2020

PREVENTION AND CONTROL OF COVID-19

ISBN 978-981-122-049-4 (paperback)
ISBN 978-981-122-050-0 (ebook for institutions)
ISBN 978-981-122-051-7 (ebook for individuals)

For any available supplementary material, please visit
https://www.worldscientific.com/worldscibooks/10.1142/11834#t=suppl

Desk Editor: Dong Lixi

Typeset by Stallion Press
Email: enquiries@stallionpress.com

Contents

Summary

This book is edited by Professor Wenhong Zhang, Director of the Department of Infectious Diseases, Huashan Hospital of Fudan University and Head of the Shanghai COVID-19 Treatment Expert Group. Professor Zhang aims to propose preventive and control measures against COVID-19 in this book. It features a comprehensive range of guidance for prevention and control measures at different places such as homes, outdoors, workplaces, etc. This book also contains scenario-based strategies, frequently asked questions, as well as efforts to debunk myths and misconceptions prevalent among the public.

This book is a valuable tool for all readers, especially those who are traveling to and/or from epidemic areas, with comprehensive, practical, concise, scientific, and targeted information on the prevention and control of COVID-19.

Contributors

Editor-in-Chief Wenhong Zhang

Editors

Xinyu Wang	Qiaoling Ruan	Feng Sun
Xian Zhou	Yang Li	Qihui Liu
Bingyan Zhang	Xuan Wang	

About the Editor-in-Chief

 **Wenhong Zhang** is Head of the Shanghai COVID-19 Treatment Expert Group, Director of the Department of Infectious Diseases, Huashan Hospital of Fudan University and Professor of Infectious Diseases. Professor Wenhong Zhang graduated from the Department of Medicine of Shanghai Medical University, and was a visiting and postdoctoral scholar in the University of Hong Kong, Harvard Medical School, and the Department of Microbiology of Chicago State University. He is currently the Director of the Department of Internal Medicine, Shanghai Medical College of Fudan University, Vice Chairman of the Internal Medicine Branch of Chinese Medical Doctor Association, Secretary General of the Infectious Diseases Branch of Chinese Medical Association, Vice Chairman of the Infectious Diseases Prevention and Control Branch of China Preventive Medicine Association, Chairman of the Infectious Diseases Branch of Shanghai Medical Association, Honorary President of the Shanghai Association of Infectious Diseases Physicians, Editor-in-Chief of *Chinese Journal of Infectious Diseases*, Deputy Editor-in-Chief of *Emerging Microbes and Infections*, and Deputy Editor-in-Chief of *International Journal of Tuberculosis and Lung Diseases*. He was awarded with many scientific and technological achievement awards such as the Chinese Medicine Award and the Shanghai Science and Technology Progress Award. In addition, he edited and co-edited nearly 20 books on

various infectious diseases, and was selected for various talent programs such New Century Talents by the Ministry of Education, Leading Talents in Shanghai, Shanghai Subject Chief Scientists, Shanghai Hundred Talents Plan and Shanghai Silver Snake Award, and won the title of Shanghai Model Worker. Under his leadership, the Department of Infectious Diseases of Huashan Hospital of Fudan University topped the National Hospital Department Ranking List for 9 consecutive years.

Professor Wenhong Zhang has been engaging in front-line clinical work for a long time and has extensive experience in the diagnosis and treatment of emerging serious infectious diseases. He participated in the prevention, control and patient treatment of the severe acute respiratory syndrome (SARS) disease in 2003; assisted Professor Xinhua Weng, the winner of the Norman Bethune Medal, to edit the first professional book on SARS in China, *SARS—An Emerging Infectious Disease*; participated in the prevention and control of Influenza A virus subtype H7N9 in 2013; and won the title of National Advanced Individual for H7N9 Prevention and Control in 2016. Some members of the expert team led by him participated in the treatment of serious infectious diseases such as the Ebola virus in Africa.

Preface

The outbreak of COVID-19 has attracted worldwide attention, and everyone is concerned with the real-time epidemic situation. From initial bewilderment or passive response, we should return to calm and rationality and gradually form a set of long-term systematic prevention and control strategies. All of the world is currently in a great battle to control the infections. There will be no doubt about the success of the battle, as we have been intensifying efforts to prevent and control COVID-19, improve screening percentage of suspected cases and enhance information transparency. To win this battle, we are relying not only on courage, but also on rationality, patience and scientific methods.

Breaking the chain of infection is the only way to control the spread of infectious diseases. However, implementation of control principles requires each of us to properly protect ourselves and actively cooperate with anti-epidemic work, in addition to relying on national prevention and control measures, so that this battle may come to an end faster.

The purpose of writing this book is to help you to protect yourself better. If all of us can protect ourselves properly, infectious diseases cannot form a closed loop of infection, and the chain of transmission will be cut off. COVID-19 is an acute infectious disease, and there is no chronic carrier of the SARS-CoV-2 virus. As humans are not the natural host of the virus, the virus will definitely be eliminated by human bodies after coexistence of 2 to 4 weeks. If the virus fails to infect other persons during this period (due to measures like wearing masks and washing hands frequently), then the virus cannot survive. The strategies we mentioned in this book may not be suitable for everyone in the world, but it can be adjusted according to the policies of your country.

As an old saying goes, "We only know the ticking of the clock, but we don't know what time it is." This battle may last for a few more weeks or even longer. However, in addition to the prevention of COVID-19, uninterrupted work and healthy lives are also our contributions to this heroic battle.

We will certainly defeat the disease that is raging. Things are neither as good as expected nor so bad as imagined! If everyone works together to avoid infecting others or being infected by others, then COVID-19 will soon be eliminated from the human society.

There are still many questions about this emerging infectious disease, and our knowledge about it is being updated every day. Omissions are unavoidable in this book due to limited writing time. We look forward to criticism and suggestions from our readers.

February 2, 2020

Learn about COVID-19 in One Minute

Overview

The 2019 novel coronavirus is now named as severe acute respiratory syndrome-coronavirus-2 (SARS-CoV-2) while the disease associated with it is referred to as COVID-19.

The virus that causes COVID-19 and the one that causes Severe Acute Respiratory Syndrome (SARS) are related to each other genetically, but they are different.

Source of infection

People can catch COVID-19 from others who have the virus, including those with no symptoms or mild symptoms.

Mode of transmission

The virus is thought to spread mainly from person-to-person through respiratory droplets produced when an infected person coughs or sneezes. These droplets can land in the mouths or noses of people who are nearby and possibly be inhaled into the lungs.

It is also possible that a person can get COVID-19 by touching a surface or object that has the virus on it and then touching his/her own mouth, nose, or possibly eyes.

The risk of catching COVID-19 from the feces of an infected person or through the air appears to be low.

Susceptible population

People are generally susceptible to COVID-19 infection. The elderly people and those with underlying conditions (e.g. hypertension, heart disorders, diabetes, liver disorders, and respiratory diseases) are expected to be at a higher risk of developing severe symptoms. Infections in children and infants have also been reported.

Incubation period

The incubation period for COVID-19 (i.e. the time between exposure to the virus and onset of symptoms) is currently estimated to be between 1 and 14 days, mostly 3 to 7 days.

Symptoms

The most common symptoms of COVID-19 are fever, tiredness, and dry cough. Some patients may have aches and pains, nasal congestion, runny nose, sore throat, or diarrhea. Some patients only have very mild symptoms such as low fever, mild fatigue, etc. Around 1 out of every 6 people who gets COVID-19 becomes seriously ill and develops difficulty breathing after 1 week of infection.

fever   fatigue   dry cough

Treatment

Possible vaccines and some specific drug treatments are under investigation. To date, there is no vaccine and no specific antiviral medicine to prevent or treat COVID-19.

However, those affected should receive care to relieve symptoms. People with serious illness should be hospitalized. Most patients recover thanks to supportive care.

Prognosis

Most people (about 80%) recover from the disease without needing special treatment. Around 1 out of every 6 people who gets COVID-19 becomes seriously ill and develops difficulty breathing. Older people, and those with underlying medical problems like high blood pressure, heart problems, or diabetes, are more likely to develop serious illness. Symptoms in children are relatively mild.

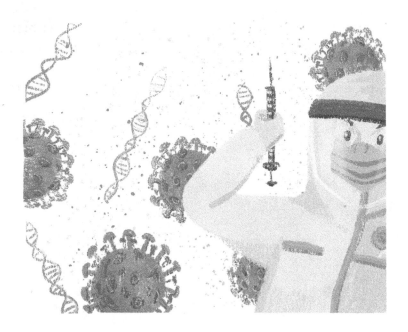

Personal Protection Keywords

Home quarantine

What is the purpose and significance of home quarantine?

The purpose of home quarantine is to prevent patients from spreading COVID-19 among the public through physical isolation, thereby avoiding the formation of second- and third-generation cases.

When there is a large number of asymptomatic close contacts or potential patients, home quarantine should be an important option to solve the problems that cannot be solved by medical institutions. If any suspected symptoms occur, you must seek medical advice. During your home quarantine, you can have leisure activities such as watching TV series, reading books, drinking tea, etc. To observe your home quarantine, you can help to prevent the spread of the virus.

Who needs to be quarantined at home?

- People who have traveled to or lived in countries or regions where local cases continue to increase within 14 days.
- People who have close contact with suspected and confirmed cases within 14 days (see Section "Close contacts" on page 26 for details).

The above-mentioned people should be quarantined at home if no suspected symptoms of COVID-19 occur (see Section "Symptoms" on page 2 for details); otherwise they should report the suspected symptoms immediately and seek medical advice (see Section "Seek medical advice" on page 49 for details).

What to do if I am quarantined at home?

Quarantine environment

- Each quarantined person should live in a well-ventilated room, and the common areas (such as kitchen, bathroom, etc.) should also be well-ventilated by leaving windows open.
- Family members should live in different rooms. If this is not possible, they should keep a distance of at least 1 meter from any patient.
- Reduce the range of activities of the quarantined person, and try to avoid instances where the quarantined person and their family members share an activity, such as dining together.
- Do not share toothbrushes, towels, tableware, toilet, bedding, clothing, etc.
- Refuse all visitors.

Nursing

- Select a person who is in good health and free of chronic illness to take care of the quarantined person.
- The caregiver should wear a mask when he/she is in the same room with the quarantined person (see Section "Masks" on page 9 for details).
- After any direct contact with the quarantined person or entering any quarantined area, the caregiver should clean his/her hands before meal preparation, before having meals, after using the toilet, and when and if contaminated with visible dirt. If the hands are free from any visible dirt, clean them with an alcohol-based sanitizer, or wash with soap and water.

Disinfection

- Clean bedroom furniture and bathroom countertops daily with chlorinated disinfectant.
- Wash the clothing and bedding of patients with hot water (60–90°C) and normal laundry detergent, and avoid mixing contaminated clothing and bedding with clean ones.
- Perform the above with disposable gloves, and wash hands before and after cleaning.

Secretion and excreta

- Respiratory secretion: When coughing or sneezing, wear a medical mask or cover mouth and nose with tissues or sleeves. Clean hands immediately after coughing or sneezing. Masks and tissues which were used to cover the mouth and nose should be discarded directly; soiled clothing should be cleaned with normal household soap/detergent and water.
- Excreta: Wear disposable gloves before handling the urine or feces of the quarantined person. Seal and discard the excreta of the quarantined person as infectious waste. Remember to cover the toilet lid before flushing the toilet.
- Pollutants: Do not reuse masks or gloves. Place all used gloves, masks, tissues and other pollutants in the patient's room, and discard them after labeling them.
- Tableware: The tableware of the quarantined person should be washed with detergent and water after use. They do not have to be discarded.

Release from quarantine

- If no suspected symptoms occur, the quarantine period ends on the 14th day of the last contact with any patient or the departure date from the epidemic area.
- If any suspected symptoms occur, you must go to any fever clinic and seek medical advice (see Section "Seek medical advice" on page 49 for details).

Masks

When do I need to wear a mask?

Wear a mask　During the epidemic period, you should wear a mask when meeting people, going to public places, entering crowded or enclosed places, taking public transportation, etc.

Wear no mask　You may wear no mask when you are alone at home or alone in an open area.

What kind of masks should I wear?

- The general public (except for medical workers or epidemic-related personnel) are recommended to wear disposable medical masks.
- Personnel working in densely populated places (such as hospitals, airports, railway stations, subways, buses, planes, trains, supermarkets, restaurants, etc.), police officers, security guards, couriers, and those who are quarantined at home and the people they live with are recommended to wear medical surgical masks, or particulate protective masks that meet N95/KN95 and above standards.
- Do not use paper masks, activated carbon masks, cotton masks, or sponge masks.

How do I put on a mask correctly?

Put on disposable medical masks/medical surgical masks as follows:

1 Hold the mask so that the nose strip is on top, and the colored side facing outwards. Place a loop around each ear.
2 Extend the folds of the mask to cover your mouth, nose and lower jaw.
3 Press your fingers down on the nose strip, and slowly mold the strip until it conforms to the shape of your nose.
4 Adjust the mask properly so that its edges fully cover your face.

A standard surgical mask contains 3 layers: the outer water-resistant layer prevents droplets from entering; the middle layer is the filter; and the inner layer that is close to your nose and mouth is used for moisture absorption.

Can I use a mask with a breather valve?

Yes   Healthy people can wear masks with breather valves to protect themselves.

No   Suspected or confirmed patients should not wear masks with breather valves, because the breather valve cannot prevent their droplets from spreading to the environment.

How long can a mask be used? Can I reuse the mask?

If you have no contact with confirmed or suspected patients, then you can appropriately reuse your masks for a longer time. However, one mask can only be used by one person. Wash your hands before wearing a mask and avoid touching the inside of the mask when wearing it.

You should immediately replace masks that are contaminated with droplets or other pollutants, or those that are deformed, damaged, or smelly.

How to store reused masks?

To reuse any mask, you should hang it in a clean, dry, and well-ventilated place, or place it in a clean, air-permeable paper bag.

You should store masks separately to avoid contact with other masks. You should also label the masks of different users. Do not wash medical masks or disinfect them with disinfectants, heating, and other methods. You should handle other kinds of non-medical masks as instructed.

How to dispose of used masks?

Masks used by the general public have no risk of COVID-19. These masks should be sealed and disposed of according to the sorting requirements of domestic waste.

Masks used by suspected or confirmed patients and their nurses should be collected and disposed of as infectious wastes. Wash hands after disposing the masks.

How to choose masks for pregnant women and children?

Pregnant women should choose more comfortable masks according to their own conditions.

Children should choose child-specific masks because of their unique anatomy and growing bodies.

Should the elderly and patients with chronic diseases wear masks?

The elderly and patients with chronic diseases such as cardiopulmonary diseases may feel uncomfortable or even worsen their conditions by wearing masks. These people should seek professional guidance from doctors.

Gloves

Do I need to wear gloves in daily life?

No The general public should wash their hands frequently in daily life, and gloves are not necessary.

Yes Medical workers, close contacts, attendants, and personnel working in crowded places should wear gloves to reduce the risk of contact transmission. However, wearing gloves is not a substitute for hand cleaning. You should also wash your hands frequently.

Goggles

Do I need to wear goggles in daily life?

No You don't need to wear goggles. In daily life and work, it is sufficient for you to keep your hands clean by washing hands frequently. You should avoid rubbing your eyes with dirty hands.

Disinfection

What are the disinfection methods?

According to the *China Diagnosis and Treatment Scheme of COVID-19 (Trial Version V)*, SARS-CoV-2 is sensitive to ultraviolet rays and heat. Heating at 56°C for 30 minutes, or using diethyl ether, 75% ethanol (alcohol), chlorinated disinfectant, peracetic acid, chloroform, and other lipid solvents can effectively inactivate the virus. However, chlorhexidine cannot effectively inactivate the virus.

Due to the lack of evidence for inactivation of SARS-CoV-2 by other disinfection methods, it is not recommended to use other methods to disinfect the virus.

What are the available disinfection methods at home?

Skin disinfection You can disinfect your skin with ethanol disinfectant.

Home environment disinfection You can wipe the surface of objects with ethanol disinfectant or chlorinated disinfectant.

Pay attention to the active ingredients of the disinfectant and its usage:

1 Ethanol is flammable. Keep it away from heat, sparks, open flames, welding and hot surfaces. Do not spray ethanol or use ethanol for large-area disinfection, otherwise a high concentration of ethanol in the air may cause a fire.
2 Pay attention to the usage of chlorinated disinfectant, especially the preparation method and dilution ratio. In particular, avoid mixing chlorinated disinfectant with other disinfectants, as a large amount of toxic gas may be generated. Refer to the product instruction for specific usage.

Disinfection of heat-resistant items   You can disinfect them by boiling for 15 minutes.

Hand-washing

When should I wash my hands?

Wash your hands after returning home from public places, after touching public goods, after covering mouth and nose with hands when coughing or sneezing, after taking off a mask, before having meals, after using toilet, after touching dirt, etc.

What should I wash my hands with?

Wash your hands with either hand sanitizer, soap and running water, or disposable alcoholic sanitizer.

How should I wash my hands?

1 Wet your hands under running water.
2 Take an appropriate amount of hand sanitizer or soap, and apply it evenly to your entire palms, backs of hands, fingers and the parts between fingers.
3 Rub your hands carefully for at least 15 seconds as follows:

- With palm to palm, close your fingers and rub hands together.
- Rub the back of your hands including the fingers.
- With palm to palm, interlace your fingers and rub hands together.
- Bend your fingers and rub finger joints in the palm of the other hand.
- Rub your left thumb with your right hand, and rub your right thumb with your left hand.
- Put your five fingertips on the palm of one hand, rotate and rub them. Repeat the same to the other hand.

4 Rinse your hands thoroughly under running water.
5 Dry your hands with a clean towel or tissue.

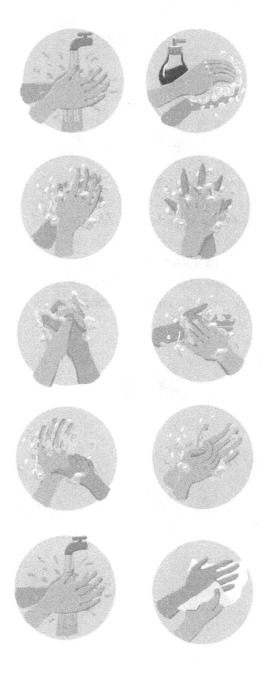

Coughing

Coughing etiquette

Cover your mouth and nose with elbows or tissues when you cough or sneeze. Never cover your mouth and nose with your hands.

Coughing and sneezing can release a lot of viruses. If your hands are contaminated with viruses and you cannot wash your hands in time, the surfaces where your hands touch, such as door handles, elevator buttons, tables and chairs, and other objects, will also be contaminated by viruses. In this case, if other people touch the contaminated surfaces and do not wash their hands in time, they may be infected upon touching their mouths, eyes, and noses with their contaminated hands.

If you cover your nose and mouth with your elbows, the viruses will stay on your clothes without contaminating the surfaces of other objects. Therefore, you should pay special attention to coughing etiquette. In addition, you should not touch your body, especially the mucous membranes in your mouth, eyes, and nose, without washing your hands.

Self-assessment of cough

See Section "Seek medical advice" on pages 46–48 for details.

Fecal-oral transmission

Can COVID-19 be transmitted by fecal-oral route?

Currently, viral nucleic acid is found positive in the feces of COVID-19 patients. However, positive viral nucleic acid in feces does not mean fecal-oral transmission. The public should not overinterpret it and thus should not panic. Transmission via aerosol, digestive tract and other routes have yet to be confirmed. Prudent practices are as follows:

1 Wash your hands before having meals and after using the toilet. See Section "Hand-washing" on page 18 for details.
2 Remember to close the toilet lid before flushing the toilet.

Elevator

Do I need to wear a mask in an elevator?
Do I risk getting infected by pressing on an elevator button?

As elevators are poorly ventilated, you should wear a mask when taking any elevator. Droplets and viruses remaining on elevator buttons may cause contact infections. It would be better if you do not use your fingers to press these buttons directly. Alternatively, you can avoid touching other parts of your body with your hands until you wash your hands after getting out of the elevator.

You may try to use the elevator less and instead opt to take the stairs to lower floors. However, as the risk of transmission is lower in non-epidemic areas, you do not need to be overly anxious. All you need to do is to wear a mask and wash your hands in a timely manner.

Air conditioning

Can I use the air conditioner?

The central air conditioning system may spread diseases. Therefore, in this period, you are advised to stop or reduce the use of the central air conditioning system. If you have to use it, you should:

1 Turn on the exhaust fans.
2 Clean and disinfect the central air conditioning system. Even split-type air conditioners should also be cleaned regularly.
3 Open doors and windows to ensure good indoor ventilation.

Pets

Can COVID-19 be transmitted by pets?

There is no evidence that pets, such as cats and dogs, can transmit COVID-19. However, after contact with pets, washing your hands with soap and water can significantly reduce the transmission risk of other common bacteria, such as *Escherichia coli* and *Salmonella*, between pets and humans. As the source and intermediate host of SARS-CoV-2 are yet to be identified, it is not recommended to raise animals of unknown origin, especially wild animals, as pets.

How to disinfect pets after they have a day out?

You don't need to disinfect your pets. Proper daily cleaning and regular pet quarantine are sufficient.

Can pets play together outdoors?

Yes.

Do pets in contact with any suspected cases need to be quarantined?

During this epidemic period, you should quarantine your pet if it came into contact with suspected cases.

Close contacts

Who are considered close contacts?

Close contacts refer to those who have one of the following contact situations with suspected and confirmed cases without taking effective precautions:

1 People living, studying, working or having close contact with such cases, such as working close to each other, sharing the same room, or living in the same house.
2 Medical staff, family members or other people who have similar close contact with such cases when diagnosing, treating, nursing or visiting such cases; people visiting or staying in a confined environment with such cases; and other patients and caregivers in the same ward with such cases.
3 People taking the same vehicle and having close contact with such cases, including attendants in the vehicle, accompanying people (family members, colleagues, friends, etc.), and other passengers and crew members who may come into close contact with such cases upon investigation and evaluation.
4 Other people who are evaluated as such by investigators.

How do I know if I am a close contact?

To identify the close contacts of suspected and confirmed cases and analyze their possibility of infection, factors such as the clinical manifestations of the cases, the contact mode with the cases, the precautions taken for contact, and the exposure to the environment and objects contaminated by the cases are considered for comprehensive judgment.

Therefore, it is the responsibility of professionals to identify close contacts, while the public only needs to truthfully provide and report relevant information. With the exception of relatives, friends and colleagues of patients, the most common close contacts are likely to be people traveling in the same vehicle with patients. Therefore, you should pay attention to your flight or train number, and the announced information about the public transportation taken by any patient. If you happen to be in the same vehicle with any patient, you must report your information and get yourself quarantined at home.

What should close contacts do?

You must report your information and get yourself quarantined at home.

See Section "Home quarantine" on page 6 for details.

COVID-19 Prevention and Control in Different Scenarios

At home

How to prevent and control COVID-19 at home?

- Exercise regularly, take adequate breaks, and get enough sleep.
- Maintain good hygiene habits: Wash hands frequently (see Section "Hand-washing" on page 18 for details); avoid touching eyes, nose, or mouth with dirty hands; and cover mouth and nose with tissues when coughing or sneezing (see Section "Coughing" on page 20 for details).
- Keep the house clean and do not share towels with family members.
- Ventilate rooms and keep them clean and tidy.
- Cover the toilet lid before flushing the toilet.
- Have thermometers, disposable medical masks, medical surgical masks or N95/KN95 masks, and household disinfection supplies ready at home.
- Minimize outdoor activities.

- Avoid close contact with people who have symptoms of respiratory diseases, such as fever, cough or sneeze.
- Avoid gatherings or visiting crowded or confined spaces.
- Avoid any contact with wild animals, poultry, and livestock.
- Pay special attention to symptoms such as fever and cough. If you have any suspected symptoms, see Section "Seek medical advice" on pages 46–48 for details.

How to disinfect at home?

See Section "Disinfection" on page 15 for details.

Can COVID-19 be prevented by taking cold medicine, *Banlangen* (isatis root) granules or vinegar fumigation?

No! Cold medicine and *Banlangen* (isatis root) granules are not effective against COVID-19, and vinegar fumigation is also not an effective method to eliminate COVID-19.

What foods are safe to eat and what are not?

- Do not consume sick animals and their products.
- Buy chilled poultry from proper channels, and thoroughly cook eggs, milk, and poultry before consuming.
- Have seperate cutting boards and knives for raw and cooked food, and wash hands between preparation of raw and cooked food.
- Even in epidemic areas, meat can be safely consumed if it is properly handled and thoroughly cooked during preparation.
- Pay attention to regular diet and balanced nutrition.

Do items purchased from supermarkets need to be disinfected?

No, all you need to do is wash your hands frequently.

Touching any objects contaminated with SARS-CoV-2 and then touching your eyes, mouth, and nose may cause indirect contact transmission. You do not need to be overly nervous due to the limited survival time of SARS-CoV-2 in vitro. Furthermore, there is a lower probability of supermarket items in non-epidemic areas being contaminated by patients' droplets.

Is take-away food safe? Does it need to be disinfected?

Take-away food is generally safe. However, you should buy food from regular stores to ensure that the meat and food are quarantined, made and processed in compliance with regulations.

If you are concerned about the risk of contact and droplet transmission caused by food delivery, you can ask the delivery personnel to leave the take-away food at the door for your picking up. After opening the package, you should wash your hands before eating the take-away food.

How to deal with express parcels from major epidemic areas or other areas?

The SARS-CoV-2 has a limited survival time after leaving the human body. When express parcels from major epidemic areas are delivered to you, the probability of SARS-CoV-2 remaining on their surfaces is relatively low, so you can receive your express parcels as usual. If you are really worried about the surface contamination of express parcels, you can open and discard the packaging materials and then wash your hands in time, especially before touching your mouth, nose, or eyes.

Can SARS-CoV-2 be killed by hot bath or steam bath?

The SARS-CoV-2 can be killed at 56°C in 30 minutes. However, such high temperature and long duration are not suitable for hot bath or steam bath generally. Excessive high temperature and long bath time may cause discomfort, such as dizziness, rapid heartbeat, or in the worst case, collapsing and fainting. Nevertheless, taking bath frequently can reduce the risk of infection.

Is it safe to use air conditioner at home?

See Section "Air conditioning" on page 23 for details.

Household split-type air conditioners will not cause viral transmission among different rooms. However, if you need to use any air conditioner, you should often open windows to ensure good indoor ventilation, and clean the air conditioner filter regularly.

Confirmed cases in community

Will SARS-CoV-2 remain on public facilities such as stair handrails and community fitness equipment?

The SARS-CoV-2 may attach to the surface of public facilities, so you should avoid touching public facilities and then touching your nose, mouth, and eyes with dirty hands. You should wash your hands immediately after you touch any public facilities.

Community managers should strengthen the cleaning and disinfection of public facilities.

What is the risk of getting infected by taking an elevator?

See Section "Elevator" on page 22 for details.

Community managers should strengtwcleaning and disinfection of elevators.

What is the risk of getting infected by the wastes of any confirmed case?

Unlikely. You should wash your hands frequently, don't touch any suspected contaminants, take effective precautions to throw garbage, and wear disposable gloves if necessary.

Going out

What should I take note of when going out?

- Wear a mask in public, especially in public transportation and crowded spaces.
- If possible, travel by foot, bike, or private car.
- Avoid any contact with people who have fever, cough, and other suspected symptoms. If you encounter such a person, you should keep a distance of more than 1 meter.
- Cover your mouth and nose with tissues or elbows when coughing or sneezing (see Section "Coughing" on page 20 for details).
- Reduce exposure to public items in public places.
- Do not touch your nose, mouth, and eyes with dirty hands.
- Wash your hands frequently, and have disposable alcoholic sanitizer, disinfectant wipes, etc. readily at hand.
- Avoid attending parties during the epidemic period.

What should I take note of when returning home?

Take off your coat → Hang your coat at the door (or a ventilated place) → Take off your mask → Wash hands → Take a shower immediately after returning home instead of taking it before sleep. If you have taken these precautions, your probability of getting COVID-19 will be very low.

Hang your coat in a specific place at the door, and keep it away from clean clothes. Without contact with any patient, there is little chance that the virus will remain on the surface of your coat. However, you should not bring your coat into your bedroom due to a large amount of dust.

See Section "Masks" on pages 12–13 and Section "Hand-washing" on page 18 for details.

Can I go for fitness activities?

See Section "Going out" on page 35 for details.

Try to avoid confined and crowded spaces, including fitness centers, during the epidemic period.

Avoid outdoor activities in crowded places. You can have some fitness activities, such as aerobics, yoga, etc. at home.

What should I take note of when taking public transportation?

See Section "Going out" on page 35 for details.

Pay special attention to wearing masks. Wash your hands after touching public items such as handrails.

How to protect people traveling in the same private car?

Passengers should wear masks, reduce their conversation, pay attention to cough or sneeze etiquette, and open windows as much as possible.

If any passenger is a suspected patient, then the interior of the private car should be thoroughly disinfected. See Section "Disinfection" on page 15 for details.

What should I take note of when taking the train/plane?

See Section "Going out" on page 35 for details.

When entering or leaving any station, you must cooperate with the staff to have your temperature taken; reduce food intake; try to avoid taking off your mask; avoid frequently touching your mouth, nose, and eyes; cover your mouth and nose with tissues or elbows when coughing or sneezing; try to keep a safe distance from others; pay close attention to the health of surrounding passengers; report any abnormalities to the staff and change your seat if possible; stay away from crowded aisles; try not to move back and forth between train carriages or aircraft cabins; and try to prepare or buy bottled water.

You should pay attention to your flight or train number, and the announced information about the public transportation taken by any patient. If you happen to be in the same vehicle with any patient, you must report your information and get yourself quarantined at home.

Returning to work

If I am from non-epidemic areas, can I return to work directly? What should I take note of?

- If you have neither contact with any patient nor have suspected symptoms, you can return to work on time in accordance with national and enterprise regulations.
- If you have contact with any patient or have any suspected symptoms, you should report your information, temporarily get yourself quarantined at home, and seek medical advice if necessary. You should decide if you should return to work according to your actual situation and professional guidance.

If I have lived and/or traveled in epidemic areas within the past 2 weeks, what should I take note of when returning to work?

- Register with the community committee or village committee as soon as possible, and reduce outdoor activities, especially activities in crowded public places.
- Monitor your health status for 14 days since the date of leaving any epidemic area. Check your body temperature twice a day, and pay attention to any respiratory symptoms such as cough, expectoration, chest distress, and shortness of breath. Where conditions permit, try to live alone or in a well-ventilated single room, and minimize your close contact with family members. See Section "Home quarantine" on page 6 for details.
- Seek timely medical advice if any suspected symptoms (including fever, cough, sore throat, chest distress, dyspnea, mild anorexia, fatigue, slight lethargy, nausea, vomiting, diarrhea, headache, palpitation, conjunctivitis, mild soreness of limbs or lower back muscles, etc.) occur. See Section "Seek medical advice" on page 49 for details.

Going to work

What is the risk of getting infected by taking an elevator?

See Section "Elevator" on page 22 for details.

What should I do when transferring files?

You should wear a mask to transfer files and then wash your hands.

Do mobile phones, telephones, and computer keyboards need to be disinfected?

Regularly disinfect office facilities. Wipe and disinfect mobile phones, telephones, and computer keyboards with alcohol-soaked cotton balls (See Section "Disinfection" on page 15 for details).

How to protect myself if I work with several people in an office?

- Ensure that your work environment is clean and hygienic, and maintain adequate indoor ventilation.
- An office in which several people work together is a public space. You should wear a mask if you are unsure whether there is any risk of infection.
- Stop or reduce the use of the central air conditioning system during this period. If you have to use it, please turn on the exhaust fans at the same time. You should also clean the air conditioners regularly.
- Open windows and doors regularly for ventilation.
- Use disinfectant regularly to disinfect office facilities, door handles, etc.
- Pay attention to hand hygiene. All places should be equipped with faucets, hand sanitizer, tissues, and hand dryers. You should develop a good habit of washing hands frequently.
- If any symptoms such as fever, fatigue, dry cough, and chest distress occur, you should stop going to work temporarily and seek timely medical advice according to your condition. See Section "Seek medical advice" on pages 46–48 for details.

Do I need to wear a mask to attend meetings?

- Always wear a mask.
- Keep a moderate distance when talking with others.
- Open your windows for ventilation.
- Reduce the number of meetings.
- Limit the duration of meetings.

Can the central air conditioning system be used in the office? If so, is disinfection necessary?

- Open doors and windows to ensure good indoor ventilation.
- Stop or reduce the use of the central air conditioning system. If you have to use it, please turn on the exhaust fans.
- Regularly clean and disinfect the air conditioners (see Section "Air conditioning" on page 23 for details).

What should I take note of regarding business travel and receiving visitors?

- All personnel should wear masks.
- Measure the body temperature of visitors and identify whether they have traveled to or lived in epidemic areas; whether they have contact with any confirmed or suspected cases; and whether they have fever, cough, dyspnea, and other suspected symptoms.
- Disinfect reception vehicles with ethanol disinfectant or chlorinated disinfectant (See Section "Disinfection" on page 15 for details).

Public places

How to protect myself when shopping in supermarkets and markets?

See Section "Going out" on page 35 for details.

Do not eat wild animals!

Avoid any contact with raw meat, stray animals, garbage, waste water, etc. in the markets, otherwise you should wash your hands as soon as possible.

How to protect myself when going to a hospital?

See Section "Seek medical advice" on page 49 for details.

How to protect myself when going to a restaurant?

Avoid dining together and try to eat at a single table alone. If you have to dine with others at the same table, do not share your meals.

Seek medical advice

When should I seek medical advice once I have suspected symptoms?

First, if you are required for home quarantine (see Section "Home quarantine" on page 6 for details), you should report the suspected symptoms immediately and seek medical advice. For notes about seeking medical advice, see Section "Seeking medical advice" on page 49.

If you are not required for home quarantine, you should carry out self-assessment as follows:

1   Your body temperature does not exceed 38°C and you are free of any symptoms like shortness of breath, dyspnea, etc.
2   You are aged below 60 and above 5.
3   You are not pregnant, chronically ill (such as lung diseases, cardiovascular diseases, chronic kidney diseases, immune diseases, etc.) or obese.

If all of the above conditions are satisfied, you should rest at home first. While at home, you should drink more water and take some cold medicine to alleviate the symptoms. In addition, you should take measures such as wearing masks, washing hands, and ventilating rooms to protect yourself and your family.

If any of the following conditions occurs, you should seek medical advice in a timely manner.

1 Your condition does not improve after observation at home for 1–2 days.
2 You recently had close contact with patients with fever and cough, visited crowded places such as hospitals, supermarkets, and farmers markets, or had a history of wildlife exposure.
3 You are elderly, pregnant, obese, or have chronic lung diseases, cardiovascular diseases, liver and kidney diseases, and other underlying diseases, or are immunocompromised.

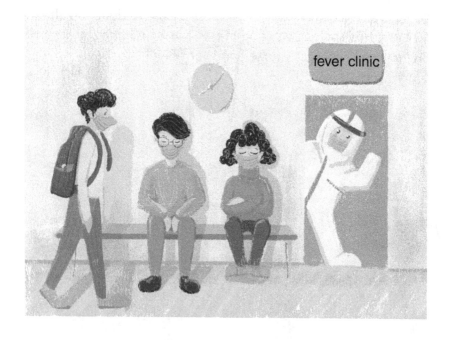

What should I take note of when seeking medical advice?

Traveling between hospital and home

- Wear a mask, and cover your mouth and nose with elbows or tissues when coughing or sneezing.
- Avoid taking subways, buses, and other public transportation, and avoid going to crowded places.
- Operators should disinfect these public transportation.

Seeking medical advice

- Tell the doctor about your travel and residence history in epidemic areas, the suspected or confirmed patients you have close contact with before developing symptoms, the people you have close contact with after developing symptoms, and cooperate with the doctor to carry out relevant investigations.
- If you suspect that you have symptoms of COVID-19, you should go directly to a fever clinic and try to minimize your activities in other areas of the hospital.
- If you must seek medical advice for other reasons, you should not walk through the fever clinic and emergency department, and avoid any contact with people who have fever, cough, and other suspected symptoms. If you encounter such a person, you should keep a distance of more than 1 meter.
- Do not stay outside after seeking medical advice. You should go home as soon as possible.

Can pregnant women have normal antenatal care?

Pregnant women can go to the hospital for normal antenatal care after taking effective precautions.

If any suspected symptoms such as fever, cough, and chest distress occur, you should report your condition to the antenatal care doctor.

Can children be vaccinated?

Based on the local epidemic situation, parents can call the vaccination agencies or Centers for Disease Control (CDC) and ask if children can be vaccinated. The offering of some vaccines can be postponed appropriately. Information released by local vaccination agencies and CDC shall prevail.

References

[1] Chinese Center for Disease Control and Prevention — COVID-19. http://www.chinacdc.cn/jkzt/crb/zl/szkb_11803/

[2] Chinese Center for Disease Control and Prevention — COVID-19 — Public Prevention Guidance: Interim Guidance for Use of Masks. http://www.chinacdc.cn/jkzt/crb/zl/szkb_11803/jszl_2275/202001/t20200129_211523.html

[3] World Health Organization — Clinical Management of Severe Acute Respiratory Infection when Novel Coronavirus (nCoV) Infection is Suspected. https://www.who.int/publications-detail/infection-prevention-and-control-during-health-care-when-novel-coronavirus-(ncov)-infection-is-suspected-20200125

[4] World Health Organization — Home Care for Patients with Suspected Novel Coronavirus (nCoV) Infection Presenting with Mild Symptoms and Management of Contacts. https://www.who.int/publications-detail/home-care-for-patients-with-suspected-novel-coronavirus-(ncov)-infection-presenting-with-mild-symptoms-and-management-of-contacts

[5] Diagnosis and Treatment Scheme of COVID-19 (Trial Version V).

[6] Clinic Guidance for Patients with Fever and Cough — Sina Weibo Official Account of Beijing Municipal Health Commission. https://m.weibo.cn/2417852083/4464198442961826

[7] Technical Guidelines for Different Groups of People on the Selection and Use of Masks for the Prevention of 2019-nCoV Infection. http://www.nhc.gov.cn/jkj/s7916/202002/485e5bd019924087a5614c4f1db135a2.shtml

[8] Chinese Medical Association — Elimination of Novel Coronavirus: "Hands" Bear the Brunt! https://www.cma.org.cn/art/2020/2/3/art_2926_32347.html

CPSIA information can be obtained
at www.ICGtesting.com
Printed in the USA
FSHW012034070720

9 789811 220494